L-780

D1608751

Searchlight
BOOKS™

What
Is Digital
Citizenship?

Smart Online Searching

Doing Digital Research

Mary Lindeen

Lerner Publications ◆ Minneapolis

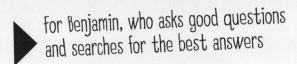

For Benjamin, who asks good questions
and searches for the best answers

Lerner Publications Company
A division of Lerner Publishing Group, Inc.
241 First Avenue North
Minneapolis, MN 55401 USA

For reading levels and more information, look up this title
at www.lernerbooks.com.

Library of Congress Cataloging-in-Publication Data

Lindeen, Mary, author.
    Smart online searching : doing digital research / Mary Lindeen.
        pages cm. — (Searchlight books. What is digital citizenship?)
    Audience: Age 8–11.
    Audience: Grade 4 to 6.
    Includes bibliographical references and index.
    ISBN 978-1-4677-9491-6 (library binding : alk. paper) — ISBN 978-1-4677-9693-4
(paperback : alk. paper) — ISBN 978-1-4677-9694-1 (pdf)
        1. Internet research—Juvenile literature. 2. Internet searching—Juvenile literature.
    3. Electronic information resource literacy—Juvenile literature. I. Title.
ZA4228.L56
001.4'202854678—dc23   2015023484

Manufactured in the United States of America
1 – VP – 12/31/15

Contents

Chapter 1

THE SEARCH BEGINS

The Internet is an amazing source of information. You can discover fascinating people, places, and facts online. Yet trying to find information you need can be frustrating. There are millions of websites. Sometimes using the Internet feels as if you're trying to use a library that has been hit by a tornado. Information is scattered everywhere!

Searching for information online can be tricky. How do you find what you're looking for?

Libraries organize information by topic and author name.

A library is usually very organized. All the books, magazines, and other items are sorted into groups. Every item has a particular place where it is kept. A library even has librarians to help you find what you need.

The Internet doesn't work that way. There is a lot of information. But it hasn't been very well organized. And there are no librarians to help you find what you're looking for either.

Librarians are happy to help you find what you are looking for in a library.

KNOWING GOOD SEARCH TERMS CAN HELP YOU FIND THE INFORMATION YOU NEED.

However, knowing a little bit about how the Internet works can help you find the information you're looking for more easily. Search tips and tools can also make your search more effective.

Defining Your Search

The first step in your search is to know what you are searching for. Searching for information is more efficient when you know exactly what you need. Being specific will narrow down the number of sites that will turn up in your search. It will take less time to find the information you want.

Make a list of words related to the topic you want to know about.

Looking up the term *goalie* or the name of a specific soccer player, such as Hope Solo (ABOVE), will turn up more results than a general search for *soccer*.

Suppose you want to know how to play soccer. There are millions of websites that have this information. It would take forever to read them all. But maybe you only need to know what a goalie does. It could take less than a minute to find that information online.

Search Engines

A search engine helps you find what you're looking for on the Internet. Search engines are software programs that copy, store, and sort information from websites. A search engine sifts through all the information it has stored. It shows you the websites that are most likely to have the information you want.

Did You Know?

You can choose the search engine you want to use on your computer. Here are some search engines that are good for kids. They are easy to use. They search for websites that have appropriate information for kids.

KidRex
http://www.kidrex.org

KidsClick!
http://www.kidsclick.org

KidzSearch
http://www.kidzsearch.com

Mymunka
http://www.mymunka.com

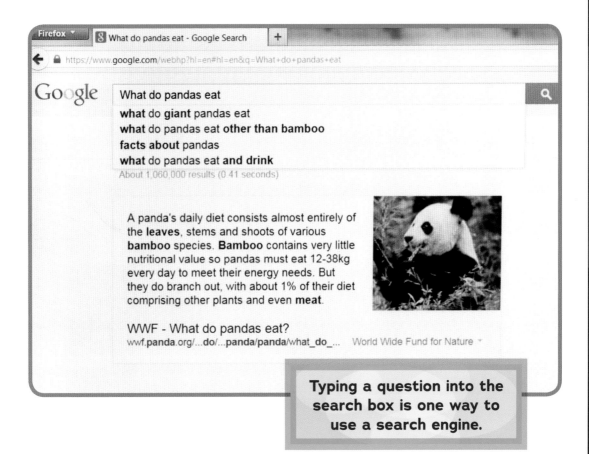

Firefox

🔲 What do pandas eat - Google Search ➕

🔒 https://www.google.com/webhp?hl=en#hl=en&q=What+do+pandas+eat

Google

What do pandas eat

what do **giant** pandas eat
what do pandas eat **other than bamboo**
facts about pandas
what do pandas eat **and drink**

About 1,060,000 results (0.41 seconds)

A panda's daily diet consists almost entirely of the **leaves**, stems and shoots of various **bamboo** species. **Bamboo** contains very little nutritional value so pandas must eat 12-38kg every day to meet their energy needs. But they do branch out, with about 1% of their diet comprising other plants and even **meat**.

WWF - What do pandas eat?
ww**f.panda**.org/...**do**/...**panda/panda**/what_do_... World Wide Fund for Nature ▾

Typing a question into the search box is one way to use a search engine.

The home page of a search engine has a search box. This is where you type in what you're searching for. You can type a question in the box. Or you can type names, phrases, or other words related to your search. These search words are known as keywords.

Tennis shoes is a popular search term. Googling this term will get you about thirty-two million results!

Using Keywords

You can use keywords to help make your search more specific. This can help you find information faster. Suppose you are looking for information about tennis shoes. Typing *tennis shoes* in the search box will show you sites about sneakers. It will also show you sites about the game of tennis and sites about all kinds of shoes.

You can narrow your search results by using quotation marks. They tell the search engine to connect the keywords in order. Type "tennis shoes" in the search box instead. Now you will see a list of only those sites that tell about tennis shoes.

Using quotes helps narrow down the results of an Internet search.

Chapter 2

HITS AND MISSES

Keywords help a search engine find websites that match your search. The search engine uses your keywords and words on each web page to decide what makes a good match.

A keyword helps define what you are looking for. What happens when you do a search for a keyword?

koala

Web   Images   Videos   Shopping   News   More ▼

About 57,300,000 results (0.36 seconds)

Koala - Wikipedia, the free encyclopedia
en.wikipedia.org/wiki/**Koala** ▼   Wikipedia ▼
The **koala** (Phascolarctos cinereus, or, inaccurately, **koala** bear) is an

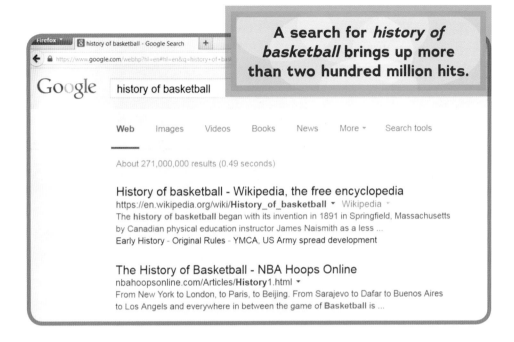

Matching sites are listed on a results page. This page shows a list of sites that use your keywords on their pages. These matching sites are called hits. The results page tells you how many hits resulted from your search.

You use the results page to go to the sites that might have the information you're looking for. The matching sites are listed on the results page according to how useful the search engine thinks each site will be for you.

Tapping or clicking on a hyperlink brings you to a new Internet location.

Hyperlinks

The websites listed on a results page are hyperlinks. Click or tap on one. That link instantly takes you to that site. This special kind of link connects one Internet location with another. These links often look different from the text around them. Sometimes they are in a different color. Sometimes they are underlined.

You can find links within websites too. They will also usually appear as words that are underlined or in a different color. Clicking or tapping on these links may take you to another part of that site. It might take you to a related site. Using links can be a helpful way to find out more about your topic.

The blue words on this website are links.

ikipedia.org/wiki/Ice_cre 🔍 ▾ 🔒 C | W Ice cream - Wikipe

Create account Lo

Article Talk   Read View source View history Search

Ice cream

From Wikipedia, the free encyclopedia

For other uses, see Ice cream (disambiguation).

Ice cream (derived from earlier **iced cream** or **cream ice**[1]) is a frozen food, typically eaten as a snack or dessert, usually made from dairy products, such as milk and cream, and often combined with fruits or other ingredients and flavours. It is typically sweetened with sucrose, corn syrup, cane sugar, beet sugar, and/or other sweeteners. Typically, flavourings and colourings are added in addition to stabilizers. The mixture is stirred to incorporate air spaces and cooled below the freezing point of water to prevent detectable ice crystals from forming. The result is a smooth, semi-solid foam that is solid at very low temperatures (<35 °F / 2 °C). It becomes more malleable as its temperature increases.

Ice cream

The Power of Persistence

Sometimes a search turns up thousands or even millions of matching sites. You won't have time to look through them all. Instead, you can try the first few since they are likely to be the most useful.

The first few links that appear in search results are often the most useful.

But what if the first few are not very useful? This happens sometimes, because some websites put many keywords on their pages, even if those keywords have little to do with the sites. They want their sites to turn up first on a results page.

In this case, looking at sites farther down the list can often help you find what you want. Perhaps the fourth site on the list—or even the fifth or the sixth—has just what you are looking for.

Keep notes on where you get your information. You can revisit those sites later if you need to.

Suppose none of the sites you visit include what you are looking for. Don't give up! There are other ways to narrow your search. Every search engine works a little differently. But following these tips and tricks should help you turn up good results on most search engines.

Check your spelling, including capital letters. A search for *china* will turn up sites related to the country in Asia (China) and fancy dishes (china). Typing *chia* as your keyword will not turn up anything about countries or dishes.

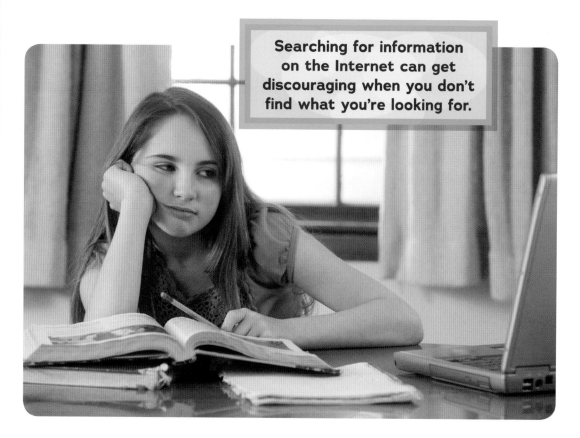

Searching for information on the Internet can get discouraging when you don't find what you're looking for.

Using specific search terms, like *Campbell's dwarf hamster*, will bring up better results than general terms, like *hamster*.

Use more keywords. Adding keywords makes your search more specific. Make sure your keywords are important to your search topic. Searching for *Wilson Elementary lunch menu* is better than *Wilson school eat*.

Use the minus symbol. Put the minus symbol in front of a keyword that you're not interested in. This is especially helpful when you search for words with more than one meaning. For instance, a rig can be part of a ship, a large platform for drilling oil, or a truck. If you only want to know about rigs that are trucks, type this in the search box: *truck rig –oil –ship*.

Chapter 3

KNOW YOUR SOURCE

You have done your search well. You've found sites that have the information you're looking for. But you still have to be careful. Not all sites are the same. You have to make sure the site you're using is factual and trustworthy.

An Internet search may pull up lots of information. But how do you know if the information you find is accurate?

A web address can tell you whom a site belongs to. A commercial site might be trying to sell you something. A site run by an organization might be trying to get you to agree with its beliefs. You have to decide if you think a site is sharing facts or opinions. A fact is information with proof that it is true. An opinion is an idea that someone believes.

Did You Know?

Look for these abbreviations in a web address. They will tell you what kind of group has created the site you're looking at.

.com = commercial: a business or group whose main purpose is to make money

.edu = education: an educational institution, like a school or a university

.gov = government: national, state, local, or tribal government in the United States

.org = organization: a business or group whose main purpose is often to help people rather than to make money

Skim and Scan

You don't have to read every word of a site to know if it has information that will be useful to you. You can look at a page briefly and then decide if you want to read the whole thing. Here are some tips for how to do this well:

Read titles and headers. These will give a general idea of the content of a page. They can help you decide if you should read more or move on.

Look for important words. Important words on a website are words that are closely related to the site's main topic. For example, *flu* might be an important word in a page about vaccinations, or shots. Important words might be in bold type. They might be underlined or in a different color. Looking for important words on a page can help you decide if you should read that page more carefully.

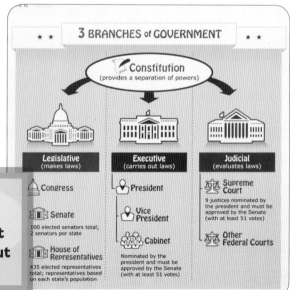

The header of this diagram on the site Kids.gov lets you know it features information about government branches.

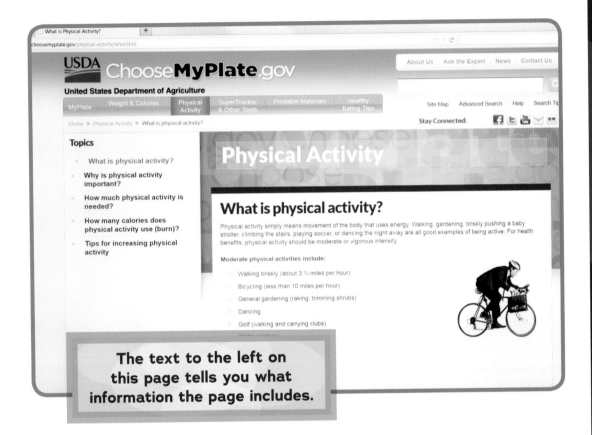

The text to the left on this page tells you what information the page includes.

Look down the left side of the page. Most people look down the left side of a web page when they are checking it out. So most web page designers put important information along the left side.

Look at the images on a page. Sometimes a chart, a graph, or a photo caption can deliver a lot of information in a very small space. Check out the images and captions on a page. They might give you the information you're looking for.

Social Media Sites

Some websites allow anyone to post and share information online. These are called social media sites. Social media sites include blogs and gaming sites. They also include sites where people post questions and other people post answers. These sites are usually not good sources for research. People can post almost anything they want. No one checks to make sure the information is true.

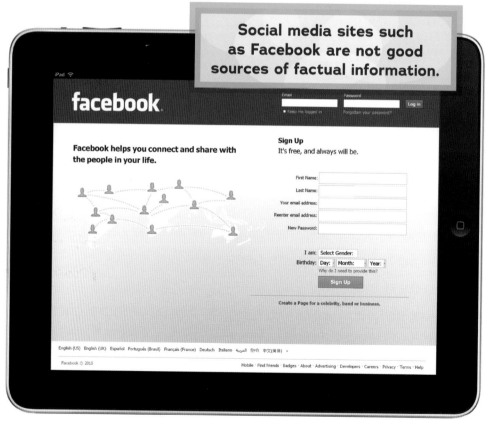

Social media sites such as Facebook are not good sources of factual information.

Wikipedia is an online encyclopedia. It often turns up near the top of a results page. But unlike many other online encyclopedias, Wikipedia pages are written by anyone who wants to write them. You can't be sure the information you read there is correct or up to date. It is not good for homework or any time your research has to be correct. It is a good place to check for quick information, though.

You should check books or reliable websites to be sure any facts you find on Wikipedia are accurate.

Safe Searching

Sometimes a search might lead you to a website that is not right for kids. It might have words or pictures that are not appropriate. Leave any site that makes you feel uncomfortable. Ask an adult you trust to help you find sites that are safe and helpful.

A trusted adult can help you find sites that are appropriate to view.

ALWAYS ASK AN ADULT BEFORE ENTERING ANY PERSONAL INFORMATION ONLINE.

Sometimes a website might ask you for personal information. It might want to know your name, age, or where you live. Never share information about yourself, your family, or your school online. Tell a trusted adult if a site asks you to share personal information. You need to protect your privacy online.

Chapter 4

THE SEARCH IS OVER

You've finally found what you've been looking for. But what do you do with it? There are several ways to use the information you find online.

> **You found some great websites. What's the next step?**

You might have looked something up to answer a question or just because you were curious. You found the information you needed. You read about it online. You shared what you learned with a friend or your family. There's nothing more you need to do. That search is over.

Sharing interesting information and fun facts with your family can make for great conversations.

Bookmark It or Print It

Your search might have led you to a website that's really interesting. You'd like to go back to that site again. You can bookmark the site. Ask an adult to help you find the bookmark option on your web browser. This tells your computer to remember that site so you can easily find it again.

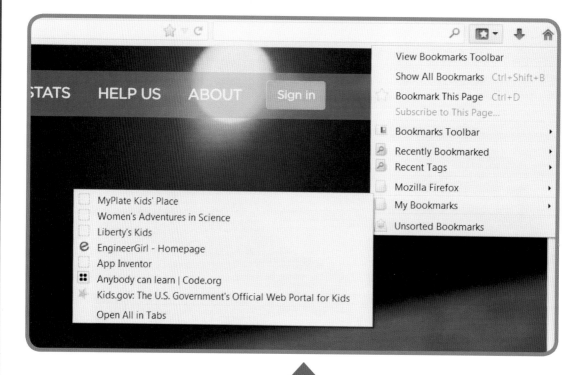

BOOKMARKING SITES YOU MIGHT VISIT AGAIN IS A GREAT IDEA.

Printing information or pictures you want to hang on to is always an option.

You might also find a website that has information you want to take with you. Maybe you want to show the information to someone else. You might want to include it in a school assignment. Or you might just want a copy for yourself. Many websites allow you to print their web pages. There might even be a printer-friendly version of the page.

Notes and Sources

Your research might be for a report or another project. You can't remember all the information you need to include. Taking notes can be very helpful. Use note cards to keep track of the important information you found online. Then you will have all the facts you need when it's time to write your report.

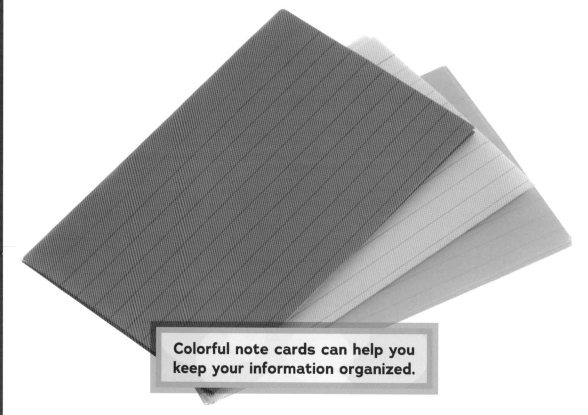

Colorful note cards can help you keep your information organized.

Carefully tracking your sources is important when you're working on projects for school.

Keep track of the sources for your notes too. You might need to prove that the information in your report is correct. You do that by showing where your facts came from. Keep track of each website's address, the date you visited the site, and the name of the site.

You might also need to prove you wrote your report using your own words. Keeping track of your sources helps protect against plagiarism. Plagiarism is a kind of stealing. It means taking credit for writing done by someone else. It is never okay to plagiarize. And it is easy for teachers to detect. Remember: If you found something online, your teacher can find it too.

Be a Good Digital Citizen

Knowing how to be safe and smart when you search the Internet is part of being a good digital citizen. It protects you from getting tricked by false or misleading information. It protects others from having their work stolen or misused. Having a world of information at your fingertips can be a challenge and a responsibility. It can also be really interesting. Make sure you stay on the smart path when you search online.

Being a smart digital researcher is part of being a great digital citizen!

Technology and the Digital Citizen

Typing keywords into a search engine is no longer the only way to find information online. You can also start a search with your own voice. Software turns the sound waves from your voice into instructions for a search engine to follow. This software allows people to tell their devices to perform a variety of tasks. You can connect to the Internet this way. You can make a phone call this way. You can turn your spoken words into printed text. This is especially helpful for people who can't type well.

Siri, which is built into some iPhones and other Apple products, is a speech recognition system with a special memory. It remembers the things you search for. It also remembers the way your voice sounds. This helps Siri understand your voice commands better. Someday we might use software like Siri to do everything from conducting online searches to driving our cars to the store.

Glossary

blog: a website or web page that contains a person's written thoughts and observations and often pictures

bookmark: to create and save an electronic link to the address of a website for quick access in the future

fact: a piece of information that is true

keyword: a significant or descriptive word used by a search engine to find relevant websites

link: a connection between one web page and another

opinion: the ideas and beliefs that a person has about something

plagiarism: stealing someone else's words or ideas and passing them off as your own

search engine: a computer software program that looks for information online at your request

software: computer programs that control the way electronic equipment works

website: a location connected to the Internet that has one or more pages on the World Wide Web

Learn More about Digital Research

Books

Fontichiaro, Kristin. *Getting Around Online.* Ann Arbor, MI: Cherry Lake, 2012. Learn how to choose good keywords, use a search engine, and conduct a successful search for information online.

Lindeen, Mary. *Smart Internet Surfing: Evaluating Websites and Advertising.* Minneapolis: Lerner Publications, 2016. Read this title to find out how to be a smart consumer of online content.

Rabbat, Suzy. *Find Your Way Online.* Ann Arbor, MI: Cherry Lake, 2010. This book encourages readers to think critically as they conduct research online.

Websites

How Search Engines Work
https://www.youtube.com/watch?v=OqcRxoAnuxg
Watch this video from PBS Kids to find out how search engines work and how to be a smart consumer of online content.

KidsHealth: What Is Plagiarism?
http://kidshealth.org/kid/feeling/school/plagiarism.html#
Find out what plagiarism is and how to avoid it.

Kidzworld: Search Engine Tutorial
http://www.kidzworld.com/article/1900-search-engine-tutorial
Learn more about how to use a search engine to find information online.

Index

Photo Acknowledgments

The images in this book are used with the permission of: © iStockphoto.com/Christopher Futcher, p. 4; © Stephen Coubrn/Shutterstock.com, p. 5; © JGI/Jamie Grill/Getty Images, pp. 6, 28, 33; © Jeff Schultz/Design Pics/First Light/Getty Images, p. 7; © Ronnachai Palas/Shutterstock.com, p. 8; © Ronald Martinez/Getty Images, p. 9; © Todd Strand/Independent Picture Service, pp. 11, 13, 14, 15, 17, 18, 21, 24, 25, 32; © Sandratsky Dmitriy/Shutterstock.com, p. 12; © Tim Robberts/ Getty Images, p. 16; © Bruce Laurance/Getty Images, p. 19; © Huntstock/Stockbyte/Getty Images, p. 20; © Thomas Barwick/Getty Images, p. 22; © pumkinpie/Alamy, p. 26; © iStockphoto. com/4774344sean, p. 27; © Alina Solovyova-Vincent/Getty Images, p. 29; © YAY Media AS/Alamy, p. 30; © Image Source/Getty Images, p. 31; © KimShanePhotos/Shutterstock.com, p. 34; © Uniquely India/photosindia/Getty Images, p. 35; © Shalom Ormsby/Blend Images/Getty Images, p. 36.

Front cover: © CristinaMuraca/Shutterstock.com, front cover.

Main body text set in Adrianna Regular 14/20.
Typeface provided by Chank.